Kamado Smoker and Grill Cookbook

The Ultimate Kamado Smoker and Grill Cookbook

James Houck

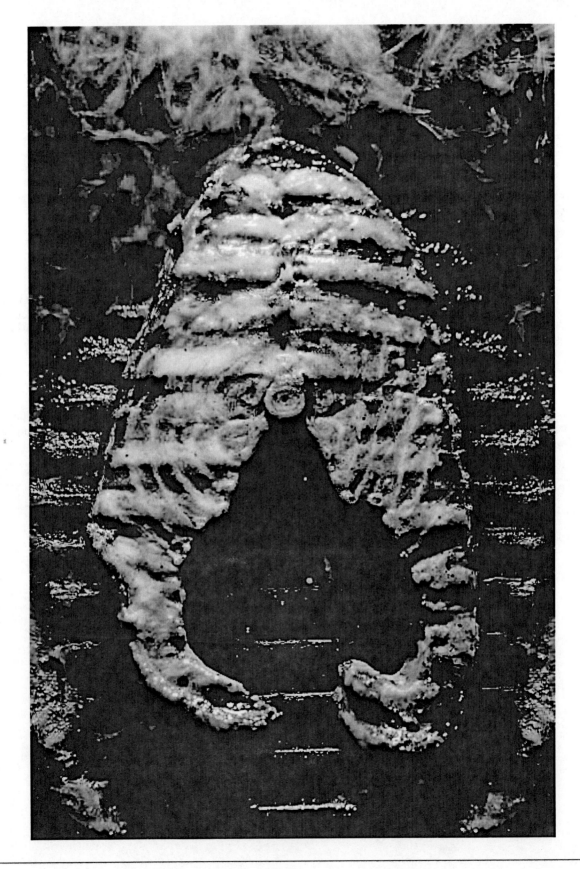

TABLE OF CONTENTS

WHAT IS A KAMADO SMOKER AND GRILL?

The word "Kamado" is a Japanese word, which means stove. Kamado Smoker and Grill is a name given to the ceramic cooker that allows you to smoke and grill the meat and vegetables.

Though the cooking pots have been a part of various ancient cultures, modern Kamado smokers come with unique features that make the usage highly pretty easy.
It is possible that you find Kamados with different styles of the ceramic outer surface. Some contain glossy ceramic surface, while others have ceramic tiles with textures. The ceramic saves the unit from getting cracked or damaged. This is what makes Kamado more effective and safer than the traditional designs.

Due to the strength and design, Kamado becomes extremely useful for various cooking purposes. Smoking and grilling is probably the most popular use of the Kamado.

However, it can also be used for baking and cooking pizzas. The ability of the vessel to handle the high temperatures brings this versatility in the cooking options.
So, you want to grill, smoke, roast or bake, anything, just put it in a Kamado.

HOW TO LIGHT THE KAMADO?

Lighting the Kamado depends on the cooking requirement. You can create a direct fire or a slow smoke to cook in the right way. Hence, there are two major types of lighting the Kamado.

WHEN YOU WANT TO SMOKE:
To light for smoking, you need to fill enough charcoal in the Kamado. Then, start the fire at the top of the collected charcoal. Putting a few pieces of charcoal over the fire will help to create the light.

The fire takes about 20 to 30 minutes to become ready for smoking. You need to leave the fire for enough time in order to get a good fire with smoke. The signs of a good smoking fire are the thin smoke that comes out of the top vent and glowing charcoal. So, you go back to your meal preparations after starting the fire and come back after 20 minutes to look for the signs.

As you start the fire at the top of the pile of charcoal, it burns from top to the bottom. The highly protected and insulated sides of the Kamado allow us to burn slowly which helps in keeping the fire for about 10 to 12 hours.

Once you see that the smoker is ready, you can put some smoking stones in it. The smoking stones provide the balance to the amount of heat attained by the food. After putting the stones inside, you need to wait for about 8 to 10 minutes. Then, your Kamado gets ready for smoking.

WHEN YOU WANT TO GRILL:

Grilling is about creating a fire that is big and burns faster. You need excess heat, so it would be better to collect as much charcoal as you can in the main chamber.

Instead of starting just one fire at the top, you need to start multiple fires to get hot glowing coal. The burning can be random for this type of cooking. There is no need to have a top to bottom burn.

You don't have to wait for 30 minutes to start grilling. Wait for a few minutes until black smoke starts coming out and the charcoal appears to be burning properly. Once that happens, you can put your grill gate and start placing your food on it.

HOW TO CONTROL THE TEMPERATURE?

Once you get a control over the temperature, the cooking gets really comfortable in Kamado. However, controlling the temperature requires you to learn a few tricks. There are usually two main sections available for you to control the temperature. One section is provided on the top, while the other is given at the bottom of the vessel.

The basic principle to remember here- the top section allows you to control the smoke that comes out and the bottom section is to let the air enter inside.

So, when you want to increase or decrease the temperature, the bottom section offers the trick. The modern designs of Kamado come with measurable controls at the bottom. You can just allow more air to go inside the chamber and it will take a few minutes to increase the temperature. The opposite function works the same manner as well.

The top section helps in clearing the smoke inside the chamber. This allows the coal to burn better by providing more oxygen in the chamber. However, extra oxygen can start a fire, which is not needed in the case of smoking. Hence, a balance is required here. You need to open the top section after a few hours in order to clear some smoke.

These adjustments are usually required at the beginning of the cooking process. After a few hours, the Kamado attains a balanced system that works on its own. You just have to keep an eye, that's it!

KAMADO COOKING

The functionality and temperature control feature of the Kamado allow you to leverage it for various cooking techniques. It is capable of providing you smoking, direct grilling, indirect grilling, roasting, and even baking environment for the food.

SMOKING

Smoking is a slow type of cooking which requires about 225°F to 275°F temperature. The food gets slow heat for a longer period of time which brings the smokiness and tenderness. The type of cooking is used for smoking meat such as pork shoulder, beef brisket, pork butts and other meat choices.

The preparation of the Kamado should be conducted to gain low heat for a long time. Then, the arrangement of the food starts the slow cooking process, which takes hours. Maintaining the low temperature for a long time is the key to get the perfection in the smoked food.

The heat retaining capacity of the Kamado becomes helpful in cooking the food without burning it.

DIRECT GRILLING

In direct grilling, the food is exposed to the fire directly. The heat from the flames works quickly on the food and gives it a nice crust on the outside while the food on the inside stays tender and sumptuous.

The fire started for grilling offers quick heat that cooks the food. So, the direct grilling is faster than smoking and used for meats and vegetables that can be cooked quickly. The hot flame while creating the crust over the meat restricts the juices and flavors from coming out.

Hence, the flavors get trapped inside the food, which makes the food really delicious. In many cooking choices, it becomes important to start grilling at high temperatures, but then, you need to gradually lower the temperature in order to get a perfect crust on the top and the tenderness inside.

INDIRECT GRILLING

In the indirect grilling method, the heat is deflected by using a grill grate or pan. It doesn't allow the food to get the direct heat coming out of the charcoal, which helps in ensuring the tenderness in the cooked food.

The juices get collected that can be used to enhance the flavors of the added ingredients.

This cooking method takes a little more time than the direct grilling. But some dishes require this cooking technique to gain the desired crispiness and juiciness together.

KAMADO SAFETY

The safety features of Kamado make it effective and reliable for people who are new to grilling and smoking. The ceramic surface on the exterior doesn't allow the high heat to come outside. Perfectly insulated, these walls keep work best in keeping the heat intact.

Not only does it provide proper cooking temperature inside, but also keeps you safe. Many times kids play around the grill, which turns into unwanted accidents. However, this is not at the care with the Kamado grill, as the outer layer doesn't get hot even at high temperatures.

However, when you are smoking or grilling, it would be wise to keep the following safety tips in mind:

OPEN THE LID CAREFULLY

This is definitely the most important to keep in mind. Opening the lid requires extreme care, otherwise, the hot coal can flash you with a big flame.

To not let it happen, you need to divide the lid opening into three steps:

1. Start by opening the two vents and wait for about 7 to 10 seconds.

2. Slowly pick the dome at the height of one inch and give it 3 to 4 seconds.

3. Now, you can completely open the dome.

These three steps keep the situation of fire surge under control. By dividing the process into slow phases, you provide enough oxygen to the fire. This is what keeps the fire from coming out towards your face.

AVOID INDOOR COOKING

One other important factor about Kamado smoker and grill is that it should be installed outdoors. Since, the cooking vessel requires an open area, it is best installed out in the open.

You also do not have to worry about the wear and tear as Kamado does not get affected by the cold weather or rain. Just cover it properly when it is not in use, and it stays in top-notch condition.

DON'T TRY TO MOVE WHEN USING

Though the outer surface of the Kamado stays cool all the time, you should not try to move it when the cooking is under process. It is, however, advisable to let the Kamado smoker and grill cool down.

USE ELECTRIC CHARCOAL

The electric charcoal starter is always a safer option when you are cooking. Any other liquid starter can become troubling for you due to the combustible nature.

The liquids can get absorbed in the ceramic surface, which can present some hazardous situations in the future. An electric starter will help you avoid such situations.

PROVIDE A SAFE ZONE AROUND THE GRILL

When you set up your grill, it is wise to keep a safe environment. Make sure that the kids and your pet aren't coming too close to the grill. For safety concerns, you should introduce a set boundary around the grill for kids.

Using Kamado becomes safer when you keep these tips in mind and avoid the silly mistakes. If you can avoid wrong handling methods, then, the design of the Kamado takes care of the rest of the general safety concerns.

KAMADO CLEANING

Proper maintenance of the Kamado smoker and grill can allow you to prepare deliciously grilled and smoked food for the lifetime. Regular maintenance along with effective cleaning will keep your ceramic grills in top-quality condition. The frequency of the cleaning depends on how many times you use them. However, cleaning is a certain requirement for sure.

So, let's talk about how to keep the Kamado smoker and grill spick and span.

THINGS YOU NEED
In order to clean your dirty grill, you need to gather a few items first.

- Get some charcoal.

- A scoop to bring out the ash from the grill.

- A brush to scrub the interior chamber.

HOW TO CLEAN YOUR KAMADO
The self-cleaning property of the Kamado smoking is a great advantage for the users. All it takes is heating, which lets the ash sit at the bottom. Then, you can simply scrub it off and get a cleaned Kamado grill.

Here are all the steps you need to conduct while cleaning your Kamado grill:

- Start by creating a fire in the grill. Make sure you create the fire at the bottom of the main chamber.

- Put the grill gate or any other heat deflector. You can also use any other cooking surface that you use.

- Now, slowly close the chamber and wait until the temperature inside reaches around 700 degrees Fahrenheit. It will take about 30 to 45 minutes for the heat to do its work. So, you need to wait that long.

- After that, you can open the upper section. Let it get cooled down now, which will take about 8 to 9 hours. So, you can organize the cleaning according to your time schedules. Leaving the heated chamber for one night will allow it to cool down.

- Next morning, you need to prepare the grill for cleaning. Bring out the accessories from the chamber, put away the heat deflector and grille gate.

- Remove the charcoal. Wearing gloves would be better to keep your hands clean.

- After cleaning the charcoal, you can now slowly take out the fire ring and the box. This will give you the space to clean all the remained ash easily.

- Now is the time when you need to use the brush to scrub all parts of the Kamado. The inner section, ceramic surface, and other sections require careful brushing.

- You will be required to scoop out the ash after every use. Any cloth can be used to bring out the leftover ash.

- Now you can start putting all the accessories back in the right place. Make sure you clean all the accessories before putting them back. Also, use cooking spray on the grill and wipe it down.

Done! Your Kamado is ready to make delicious dishes with you again. This type of deep cleaning is required in every 6 months, so that, the food can get proper heat and all the advantages of Kamado.

The cleaning process allows the Kamado to retain its moisture holding capacity and keeps the temperatures precisely controlled. As a result, you get more and more praises for your delicious cooking.

KAMADO CONVERSION CHART

When you start learning recipes, the measurements become troubling sometimes. You get the measurements of the ingredients in different forms. Then, the guesswork happens and you end up adding either too much or too less of the ingredients. These confusions are common, which makes people feel anxious about using the recipes.

The only way to resolve this problem is by having a conversion chart for Kamado. The conversion charts definitely help you keep the ingredients in the right quantity and ensure the perfect taste according to the recipe.

So, have a look at the following Kamado conversion charts for a flawless cooking.

CONVERSION CHART FOR CUPS

When you see the measurements of the ingredients given in "number of cups", it doesn't really give you the exact value. Which is why it becomes confusing and difficult to convert them into tablespoon and teaspoon values.

This chart will help you do that.

CUPS	TEASPOONS	TABLESPOONS
1 C	48 Tsp	16 Tbsp
¾ C	36 Tsp	12 Tbsp
2/3 C	32 Tsp	11 Tbsp
½ C	24 Tsp	8 Tbsp
1/3 C	16 Tsp	5 Tbsp
¼ C	12 Tsp	4 Tbsp
1/8 C	6 Tsp	2 Tbsp
1/16 C	3 Tsp	1 Tbsp

CONVERSION CHART FOR BUTTER

Butter is an important ingredient when you are grilling. But there are multiple ways to describe the measurements of the butter, which may create confusion.

To avoid that, you can leverage the following chart.

CUPS	TABLESPOONS	STICKS	WEIGHT (G)	WEIGHT (OZ)
2 C	32 Tbsp	4 stick	454 g	16 oz
1 ¾ C	28 Tbsp	3 ½ stick	398 g	14 oz
1 ½ C	24 Tbsp	3 stick	341 g	12 oz
1 ¼ C	20 Tbsp	2 ½ stick	284 g	10 oz
1 C	16 Tbsp	2 stick	227 g	8 oz
¾ C	12 Tbsp	1 ½ stick	170 g	6 oz
½ C	8 Tbsp	1 stick	113 g	4 oz
¼ C	4 Tbsp	½ stick	57 g	2 oz

CONVERSION CHART FOR WEIGHTS OF INGREDIENTS

There are a few ingredients most commonly used in many dishes. Both smoked and grilled dishes require these ingredients.

Hence, a conversion chart for their weight would be perfect to make cooking convenient for you.

INGREDIENT	2 Tbsp	¼ Cup	1/3 Cup	1/2 Cup	2/3 Cup	¾ Cup	1 Cup
FLOUR	15 g	30 g	40 g	60 g	80 g	90 g	120 g
SUGAR	25 g	50 g	65 g	100 g	130 g	150 g	200 g
CONFECTIONER'S SUGAR	13 g	25 g	35 g	50 g	70 g	75 g	100 g
BROWN SUGAR	23 g	45 g	60 g	90 g	120 g	135 g	180 g
CORN MEAL	20 g	40 g	50 g	80 g	100 g	120 g	160 g
CORN STARCH	15 g	30 g	40 g	60 g	80 g	90 g	120 g
UNCOOKED RICE	24 g	48 g	65 g	95 g	125 g	140 g	190 g
UNCOOKED MACARONI	17 g	35 g	45 g	70 g	90 g	100 g	140 g
UNCOOKED COUSCOUS	22 g	45 g	60 g	90 g	120 g	135 g	180 g
UNCOOKED OATS	11 g	22 g	30 g	45 g	60 g	65 g	90 g
TABLE SALT	40 g	75 g	100 g	150 g	200 g	230 g	300 g
BUTTER	30 g	60 g	80 g	120 g	160 g	180 g	240 g
VEGETABLES SHORTENING	24 g	48 g	65 g	95 g	125 g	140 g	190 g
CHOPPED VEGETABLES AND FRUITS	20 g	40 g	50 g	75 g	100 g	110 g	150 g
CHOPPED NUTS	20 g	40 g	50 g	75 g	100 g	110 g	150 g
GROUND NUTS	15 g	30 g	40 g	60 g	80 g	90 g	120 g
BREADCRUMBS	8 g	15 g	20 g	30 g	40 g	45 g	60 g

GRILLED POT ROAST WITH VEGETABLES
INGREDIENTS TO PICK:

Pot Roast

Beef Broth

Potatoes

Celery

Onion

Carrots

Fresh ground black pepper

Brown gravy mixture, about 3 tablespoons

Kosher Salt

COOKING DIRECTIONS:

1. Burn the exterior surface of the pot roast at the temperature of 350 degrees.

2. Use ground pepper and kosher salt for the seasoning of the roast.

3. Now, after the complete burning of the meat surface put it in Kamado for grilling.

4. Include potatoes, carrots, onion and celery in it to cook them along with the meat.

5. Keep the temperature around 350 degrees and cook for about three to four hours. Adjust the cooking time period according to the size of the pot roast you have.

6. Monitor the amount of beef broth and add more if required during the cooking time.

GRILLED SALMON
INGREDIENTS TO PICK:

Salmon steaks or filets- 1 pound and with 1 inch thickness

Dry sherry- 2 tablespoons

Soy sauce- 2 tablespoons

Brown sugar- 1 tablespoon

Garlic cloves- 2

Minced fresh ginger- 1 tablespoon

Dry ginger- 1 teaspoon

Sliced green onion- 1

COOKING DIRECTIONS:

1. Start by cleaning the salmon with the help of mildly cold water. Use a clean towel to pat dry the fish.

2. Take a bag that has zip lock. Put sherry, ginger, brown sugar, garlic, and soy sauce in the bag.

3. Now, insert the salmon inside the bag and seal it. Then, keep the bag under refrigeration for about 45 to 60 minutes.

4. In the meantime, prepare your Kamado for the grilling. Set the grill on 275° to 350°F and put grill stones over the grilling grate.

5. About a 2 or 3 handfuls of chips will help the charcoal to get smoked better. You can close the upper lid and wait for it to get prepared.

6. When the Kamado is ready for grilling, add the fish over the cooking grate.

7. Grilling will take about 9 to 10 minutes. You can check whether the fish has been cooked or not by using a fork. If the fish flakes comfortably, then, it is time to remove it from the grill.

8. Shift the salmon from the grill to the plate. Serve it with onion garnishing.

GRILLED TERIYAKI CHICKEN
INGREDIENTS TO PICK:

Skin-on chicken breast halves, 3 to 4 pounds

Crushed garlic, 2 cloves

Soy sauce, ¾ cup

Fresh ginger root, 1 tablespoon

Ground sea salt, ½ teaspoons

White wine or sherry, ¼ cup

COOKING DIRECTIONS:

1. Wash the chicken breasts in mildly cold water and pat dry it with a clean towel.

2. Set the Kamado for grilling at about 350 degrees F. Give it about 20 to 30 minutes to get ready for grilling.

3. Use stones to deflect the heat.

4. Take a large bowl to prepare a mixture of soy sauce, garlic, ginger, wine or sherry, and salt.

5. Include chicken in the mixture and use your hands to rub the mixture over the breasts. Leave it to marinate for about 3 to 5 hours.

6. When Kamado is ready, take the chicken breasts and place them on the grill. Put it in the lower grill surface and make sure that the skin side is towards the grill surface.

7. Grill the chicken till you see the juices and the chicken starts looking opaque. Make sure you turn the breasts after every 5 to 6 minutes. You can use the meat thermometer as well to ensure the 175 to 180 degree F temperature in the thickest part of the chicken.

8. Now, you can remove the chicken from the grill. Give it about 10 to 15 minutes and then serve.

BACON WRAPPED CHICKEN KABOBS
INGREDIENTS TO PICK:

Chicken tenders

Bacon, thin-sliced

Any seasoning you prefer

Any barbeque sauce you like

Skewers for barbeque

COOKING DIRECTIONS:

1. Prepare your Kamado grill by heating and placing a drip pan at the bottom of the assembled shelf. The pan will allow you to safely collect the grease of the bacon.

2. Make sure that the Kamado is at 400 degrees F to grill the chicken and bacon.

3. In the time when the grill is heating up, you can cut the chicken tenders. Prepare one-inch pieces to easily skew them.

4. Now, use a thread of one-inch length to bind the bacon. Take one end of the bacon and then add one chicken piece. Make sure you use the thread to wrap the bacon around the chicken.

5. Do the same with other bacon and chicken pieces.

6. Prepare skewers with 5 to 6 pieces of chicken in each.

7. Carefully adjust the chicken in the skewer and place it on a sheet.

8. Now, Sprinkle the seasoning on each side of the skewers.

9. Grill must be hot by now. You can place the skewers on it.

10. Let them get grilled for about 15 to 20 minutes, then, turn them to cook the other side. Keep looking for the brown spots in bacon. Cook until the chicken starts looking opaque. It should take about 20 to 25 minutes.

11. Shift the kabobs from the grill and use a soft brush to add barbeque sauce on them. They are ready to serve now!

HOT STEAK SANDWICH
INGREDIENTS TO PICK:

Hoagie rolls, 4

Swiss cheese, 4 slices

Slices onion, 1

Roasted seeded and stemmed chili, 2

Vegetable oil, 3 tablespoons

Dried thyme, ½ teaspoon

Beef, 1 pound, sliced pieces of 2 inch length

Onion powder, ½ teaspoon

Garlic powder, ½ teaspoon

Black pepper, ½ teaspoon

Chili powder, 1 teaspoon

Salt, 1/2 teaspoon

COOKING DIRECTIONS:

1. Take a bowl to prepare a mixture of pepper, chili powder, salt, onion powder, thyme, and garlic powder.

2. Add the strips of beef and cover the strips with the coating of the mixture.

3. Add seasoning mixture to the meat.

4. Prepare your Kamado grill for medium-high temperature grilling. Add 1 ½ tablespoons of oil over the grilling pan.

5. When the oil starts shimmering, put the beef on it and grill for 2 to 3 minutes.

6. Set aside the grilled meat, and start working on the chili and onions. Use the 1 ½ tablespoon of oil to mildly cook onions and chili until the onion gets light brown. It will take about 5 minutes only.

7. Separate the meat into 4 portions and layer them over the 4 rolls.

8. Add the layers of onion and chili and place the cheese slice on it.

9. Use a baking sheet to melt the layer of cheese slice by broiling. The rolls are ready to serve now.

GRILLED CHICKEN WITH MANGO AND PEACH SALSA
INGREDIENTS TO PICK:

Chicken breasts, 6 ounces, boneless and skinless

Fresh mango, 1 cup, chopped

Fresh peaches, 1 cup, chopped

Lime juice

Red bell pepper, ½ cup, chopped

Sea salt

Sliced red onion, ¼ cup

Basil leaves, ¼ cup

Olive oil, 2 teaspoons

COOKING DIRECTIONS:

1. Take a bowl to mix mango and pieces of peaches with lime juice, pepper, and onion. Now, start preparing your Kamado for grilling. Set it at a temperature of about 325 degrees F.

2. In the meantime, take your chicken and rub it with olive oil, seasoning and salt as well. Place the grill grate over the Kamado and let it get heated for about 1 to 2 minutes.

3. Put the chicken over the platform and grill it for about 20 to 30 minutes. Shift the chicken from the grill to a plate. Pour lime juice all over it.

4. Add basil into the already prepared mango and peach salsa and place the salsa over the cooked chicken. Now, serve and enjoy.

GRILLED SHRIMP WITH CRAB STUFFING
INGREDIENTS TO PICK:

Large shrimp, 18 to 20 pieces, peeled and deveined

Crabmeat, 1 lb

Bacon, 1 packet, thin cut

Barbeque Rub

COOKING DIRECTIONS:

1. Prepare the Kamado for grilling and set the temperature at 400 degrees F.

2. Use a little amount of oil to grease the cooking platform. Carefully cut open the shrimp from the back. Make sure you don't cut it into two pieces.

3. Take one spoon of crabmeat and fill it inside each sliced shrimp.

4. Now, use bacon and toothpick to secure the stuffed shrimp. Wrap the bacon around the stuffed shrimp and protect it with a toothpick.

5. Sprinkle a little bit of barbeque rub and leave it for about 4 to 6 minutes.

6. Directly put it over the cooking platform and let it cook for about 4 to 5 minutes. Keep switching the sides to ensure balanced cooking.

7. Now, let it get cooled for about 15 minutes and serve.

GRILLED OYSTERS
INGREDIENTS TO PICK:

Fresh oysters, about a dozen

Roasted garlic basil and parsley butter, about 6 tablespoons

Chives, 3 tablespoons, chopped

Lemon slices of one lemon

COOKING DIRECTIONS:

1. Prepare the Kamado on the grilling mode at a temperature of about 425 degrees F.

2. Bring out the roasted butter in a bowl and let it get softened.

3. Use an oyster knife to slowly open the oysters.

4. Get rid of the top and flat shell. Also, remove the discards.

5. Shift the oysters over the cooking grid of the grill. Use the bowl side of the shell while placing.

6. Now, take this grid to the Kamado grill and introduce ½ tablespoon of the roasted garlic basil and parsley butter on each of the oyster.

7. Close the Kamado's lid and wait for about 5 minutes. The oysters will start bubbling and the butter will melt completely.

8. As you see the caramelization on the oyster shells, shift them from the grill to the serving plate. Pour some lime juice and use chives to garnish the plate.

GRILLED BABY ARTICHOKES WITH SPICY HOLLANDAISE SAUCE

INGREDIENTS TO PICK:

Baby artichokes, 1 package

Hollandaise sauce, 1 package

Lemon, 1

Chili powder, ½ teaspoon

Olive oil, according to the need

Sea salt

COOKING DIRECTIONS:

1. Prepare your Kamado and set it at 425 degrees F.

2. Take 2 cups of water in a bowl and squeeze the lemon in it.

3. Take out the artichokes and wash them properly. Peel to get the equal sizes and then cut them into small half inch pieces. Now, place all the chokes in the lemon water. The lemon water stops the oxidation of the chokes.

4. Your Kamado must be ready by now. You can put the chokes on a pan and oil the cut surface. Put the pan on the grill and let it get grilled for about 4 to 5 minutes.

5. Now, oil the top part and change the side to cook for another 4 to 5 minutes.

6. After grilling, shift the chokes into a bowl and quickly cover it. Use a plastic wrap to cover the chokes. Covering the chokes for 10 minutes will steam it properly.

7. Take out the hollandaise sauce from the package and heat it.

8. Plate the grilled artichokes and pour the sauce over it. Ready to serve!

TANGY GRILLED GROUPER
INGREDIENTS TO PICK:

Grouper, 2 fish fillets

Lemon juice, 1 tablespoon

Olive oil, 1 ½ teaspoons

Minced fresh rosemary, 1 ½ teaspoons

Dash pepper

Salt, ¼ teaspoon

Tomato, ¼ cup, diced and seeded

Green onion, 1 tablespoon, chopped

Minced fresh basil, 1 tablespoon

Red wine vinegar, 1 ½ teaspoons

Grated orange peel, ¼ teaspoon

COOKING DIRECTIONS:

1. Take a sealable bag to prepare the mixture of rosemary, salt, pepper and lemon juice

2. After mixing all the ingredients, include the fish as well. Seal the bag and put it to refrigerate for about one hour.

3. Now, drain and remove the marinade.

4. Get your Kamado ready for grilling. Set the temperature at about 350 degrees F and place a perforated cooking platform over it.

5. Bring out the fish from the refrigerator and shift it to the cooking platform for grilling. Keep the direct cooking go on until the fish starts flaking easily. You can use a fork to see if the fish flakes.

6. Combine tomato, olive oil, basil, red wine vinegar, grated orange peel and other ingredients in a pan. Cook it over a medium heat for a few minutes until the sauce gets ready.

7. Now, serve the fish with this tangy sauce.

CHORIZO STUFFED GRILLED DUCK WITH APPLE SAUCE
INGREDIENTS TO PICK:

Duck breasts, 4

Black pepper, 2 tablespoons

Salt, 2 tablespoons

Paprika, 2 tablespoons

Apple brandy, ½ cup

Sugar, 2 tablespoons

Apple juice, 1 cup

Chorizo sausage, 2 links

Sage leaves, 3, chopped

Chicken stock, ¾ cup

Parsley, 2 tablespoons, chopped

Cornbread, 1 ½ cups

Extra virgin olive oil, 1 ½ tablespoons

Salt and pepper for the stuffing preparation

COOKING DIRECTIONS:

FOR APPLE SAUCE:

1. Take a frying pan to add apple juice, sugar, and apple brandy.

2. Cook it until the boiling and gradually decrease the heat to 300 degrees F.

3. Balance stir the sauce for about 20 minutes and set aside to reduce the temperature.

FOR DUCK BREASTS:

4. Put the olive oil in the pan and add chorizo. Balance the cooking by regular stirring.

5. Include chicken stalking and cook till it starts boiling.

6. Now, set the pan aside from the cooking platform and completely cover the cooked stuffing with cornbread, sage and chopped parsley.

7. Add the salt and pepper according to your taste and leave it to get cool.

8. Prepare your Kamado for grilling at a temperature of about 375 degrees F.

9. Take a sharp and small knife and carefully create a pocket in each duck breast.

10. Now, stuff the cooled chorizo stuffing in the breasts.

11. Use black pepper and paprika to season the breasts all over.

12. This preparation will allow the time for the Kamado to get ready. Now, you can put the fat side of the breast over the grill and directly cook it for about 9 to 10 minutes.

13. When you see a golden brown color of the duck breasts, shift it to the serving plate.

14. Give a light brush stroke of the applesauce over the breasts and leave it for 8 minutes. Now, it is ready to serve.

GRILLED MAHI-MAHI FISH
INGREDIENTS TO PICK

Mahi-Mahi fillets, 4 of about one-inch thickness

Fish base, 1 tablespoon

Sesame oil, 1 ½ tablespoons

Soy sauce, ½ cup

Honey, 1 teaspoon

Sesame seeds, 2 teaspoons

Honey, 1 teaspoon

COOKING DIRECTIONS:

1. Prepare the Kamado for grilling at a temperature of about 400 degrees of F.

2. Take a bowl of medium sized bowl with medium depth.

3. Add soy sauce, fish base, honey, garlic powder, and sesame oil in the bowl.

4. Include the fish fillets in the mixture and let it get marinated for about 20 to 30 minutes.

5. After 30 minutes, shift the fish fillets directly over the grill for about 4 to 5 minutes.

6. Now, change the side and grill again for about 4 to 5 minutes.

7. Serve it on the plate and garnish it with sesame seeds.

SKEWED CHICKEN THIGHS WITH GRILLED VEGGIES
INGREDIENTS TO PICK:

Chicken thighs, 2 pounds, boneless, skinless

Lime juice, 1/3 cup

Garlic cloves, 4, minced

Extra virgin olive oil, 1/3 cup

Salt, 2 teaspoon

Brown Sugar, 1 tablespoon

Ground cumin, 1 ½ teaspoon

Black pepper, 1/8 teaspoon

Sweet onion, 1 large, peeled and cut into cubes

Red bell pepper, 1 large, seeded and cut

Green bell pepper, 1 large, seeded and cut

Cilantro

COOKING DIRECTIONS:

1. First of all, you need to prepare the marinade by mixing lime juice, sugar, salt, garlic, cilantro, black pepper, and cumin. Combine all the elements together nicely.

2. Cut the pieces of the chicken in a 1-and-a-half-inch chunk.

3. Take a sealable bag to put the chicken thigh pieces along with the prepared mixture. Seal the bag and leave it to refrigerate for about 2 to 6 hours.

4. Use skewers to carefully skew the chicken, tomato, red pepper, green pepper, and onion pieces in an alternating manner. Prepare multiple skewers like this.

5. Prepare the Kamado for cooking at the temperature of about 400 degrees F.

6. Grill the chicken and veggies for about 4 to 5 minutes.

7. After cooking, let it get cooled down for about 5 minutes, then, serve.

SMOKY MEATLOAF
INGREDIENTS TO PICK:

Ground beef, 2 pounds

Celery, 2 stalks, diced into small pieces

Onion, 1 cup, diced in small pieces

Breadcrumbs, 2 cups

Garlic cloves, 3, minced

Carrot, 1, grated

Red wine, ½ cup

Eggs, 3

Soy and vinegar sauce, 2 tablespoons

Red wine vinegar, 1 teaspoon

Rosemary, 1 tablespoon, minced

Salt, 2 tablespoons

Paprika, 1 tablespoon

Ketchup, ½ cup

COOKING DIRECTIONS:

1. Get your Kamado ready for smoking at 350 degrees F.

2. After that, start by cooking carrot, celery, and onions at a low temperature for about 14 to 16 minutes. Cook until the veggies start looking translucent.

3. Without removing the veggies add garlic after 16 minutes and let it cook for 2 minutes more.

4. Now, take a mixer to mix ground beef and the eggs one by one. Include wine, seasoning, and herbs. Don't add the ketchup yet. Prepare small patties of this mixture.

5. Take a pan and brush butter on it to put the meat patties.

6. Now, place it in the Kamado to cook for about 20 minutes.

7. After 20 minutes, you can take the meatloaf and pour ketchup all over the top section. Now, smoke it for 10 minutes more in order to merge the ketchup with the meatloaf.

8. The smoky meatloaf is ready to get served.

SMOKED APPLES WITH VANILLA ICE CREAM
INGREDIENTS TO PICK:

Firm sweet apples, 6

Dark brown sugar, ¼ cup

Unsalted butter, 6 tablespoons

Dried currant, ¼ cup

Ground cinnamon, ½ teaspoon

Shortbread crumbs, ¼ cups

Cinnamon sticks, 4 pieces

Vanilla extract, 1 teaspoon

Nutmeg, ¼ teaspoon, grated

Marshmallows, 4, halved

Vanilla ice cream

COOKING DIRECTIONS:

1. Use a melon baller to carefully create a cavity in the apples. Make sure you don't create a hole in the apples.

2. Mix brown sugar and butter together and cream them to get a fluffy and light texture.

3. Take cookie crumbs, currants, nutmeg, cinnamon and vanilla and beat them together. Now, use a small spoon to fill this mixture evenly inside the cavity of the apples.

4. Place the cinnamon stick on the mixture and stick a half piece of marshmallow on the cinnamon stick.

5. Now, place the apples in an organized manner over the grill rings with the help of aluminum foils.

6. Set your Kamado at about 300 degrees F and smoke it for about 1 to 1 ½ hours.

7. When start feeling that the sides of the apples have become a little squeezable, take them out.

8. Serve the hot apples with the chilled vanilla ice cream.

TWICE SMOKED POTATOES
INGREDIENTS TO PICK:

Baking potatoes, 4 large pieces of about 14 ounces

Ground black pepper

Sea salt

Melted butter, 2 tablespoon

FOR STUFFING:

Unsalted butter, 4 tablespoons, thin slices

Bacon strips, 4, cut in ¼ inches crosswise

Scallions, 4 tablespoons, chopped

Sour cream, ½ cup

Cheddar cheese, 2 cups

Smoked paprika

COOKING DIRECTIONS:

1. Prepare the Kamado for smoking by adding some hardwood. Make sure that the preheat temperature is about 400 degrees F.

2. Use a vegetable brush to properly clean the potatoes. Make some holes on them with the help of a fork and then season carefully with pepper and salt.

3. Now, smoke the potatoes for about 1 and a half hour in order to get a soft and tender texture.

4. During the time of potato smoking, you can take your bacon skillet to fry and drain it.

5. After the first smoking is completed, shift the potatoes on a cutting board. Now, you need to start cutting the potatoes in half lengthwise.

6. After cutting them, scoop out the potato by leaving a ¼ inch to use as a shell.

7. Collect the scooped out potato in a bowl and mash it together.

8. Take bacon, melted butter, cheese and the scallions and stir them together. Also include the salt, pepper, and sour cream for the taste.

9. Mix it all in the mashed potato and stuff it in the shells of potato.

10. Put a slice of butter over it and some paprika.

11. Finally, smoke the potatoes again in a preheated temperature of 400 degrees F for about 25 minutes. And serve it hot.

SMOKED SPARERIBS WITH HOMEMADE SAUCE
INGREDIENTS TO PICK:

Spareribs, 2 racks, peeled

FOR RUB:

Kosher salt, 4 tablespoons

Paprika, 4 tablespoons

Sugar, 4 tablespoons

Black pepper, 2 tablespoons

Chili powder, 2 tablespoons

Onion powder, 2 tablespoons

Dried thyme, 2 tablespoons

Dried oregano, 2 tablespoons

FOR SAUCE:

Dried oregano, 1 teaspoon

Sugar, ½ cup

Dried thyme, ½ teaspoon

Kosher salt, 2 teaspoons

Garlic, 1 teaspoon, granulated

Black pepper, 1 teaspoon

Molasses, 1 cup

White vinegar, ½ cup

Cayenne Pepper, 1 teaspoon

Yellow mustard, ¾ cup

Tomato ketchup, 1 cup

COOKING DIRECTIONS:

1. You need to first start by working with the ingredients provided for the Rub. Mix all of them together and rub them on all sides of the ribs.

2. Fold the ribs in a foil and leave them for the night to refrigerate.

3. On the second day, you can prepare the Kamado for smoking process. Add charcoal and set the Kamado at a temperature of about 245 degrees F.

4. After the Kamado gets ready, you need to smoke the ribs for about 3 hours. Then, again conduct the cooking for 2 hours by wrapping the ribs in a foil.

5. When the cooking is done, you can take the ribs out and let it rest for about 1 hour.

6. To prepare the sauce, you need to mix all the ingredients given for the sauce. Cook it in a dim heat until a thick sauce gets ready.

7. Pour the sauce all over the ribs when you are ready to serve.

SMOKED RIBS WITH APPLE AND HONEY
INGREDIENTS TO PICK:

Ribs, 3 slabs, cleaned and cut in half

Honey, 1 cup

Apple juice, 1 ½ cup

Dry Rub, 1 cup

Honey sauce, 2 cups

COOKING DIRECTIONS:

1. Use the Rub all over the ribs. Make sure that most of the Rub gets in the meaty side of the ribs. Leave the rubbed ribs for about 45 minutes at room temperature.

2. Prepare the Kamado for smoking at 325 degrees F until the ribs get ready. Make sure there is enough space for all 3 slabs.

3. Smoke for about 1 ½ hours. Then, shift the ribs on a pan and rub it with honey on each side.

4. Now take the ribs and place them in a pan with enough depth to pour 1 inch of apple juice in it.

5. Use foil to cover the pan and start cooking for extra 1 hour. You can add more apple juice during cooking if you feel like. But make sure you keep on monitoring the tenderness of the ribs time to time. You can use a toothpick for that.

6. After getting a tender texture, you can take them out, wrap them in different foils and refrigerate for about 1 or 2 days.

7. At the time of serving, a little bit of grilling in medium heat prepares the ribs. A few minutes of cooking with regular changing the sides, and brush the honey on each side as well.

8. Cut the ribs and serve.

PORK LOIN SANDWICH
INGREDIENTS TO PICK:

Pork loin, 7 lb, center cut

Buns

Seasoning

Spanish onions, 2, cut into thin rings

Barbeque sauce

Flour, 2 cups

Buttermilk, 2 cups

Kosher salt, 1 teaspoon

Cayenne pepper, ½ teaspoon

Black pepper, 1 tablespoon

Vegetable oil

COOKING DIRECTIONS:

1. Prepare your Kamado for the smoking at a temperature of about 250 degrees F.

2. During the time when the Kamado gets ready, you can work on the seasoning. Rub the seasoning all over the pork loin and leave it at the room temperature for about half an hour.

3. Now, you can start cooking the pork loin. The cooking time is until the internal temperature gets about 160 degrees F.

4. After that, you can simply shift the pork loin and refrigerate for cooling. The cooling will make it easier for you to slice the pork in thin slices. Also, you need to give at least 1 hour to the onion to get soaked in buttermilk.

5. Mix all the ingredients such as flour, black pepper, cayenne, kosher salt. Use this mixture to toss the soaked onion.

6. Preheat the vegetable oil of one-inch depth in the pan. Now, cook the onions till you attain the golden brown color.

7. Take 4 to 5 minutes to sauté the slices of the pork with the barbeque sauce.

8. Finally, you can toast the buns and add pork slices and onion rings.

SMOKED TURKEY (WHOLE)
INGREDIENTS TO PICK:
Turkey, 12 to 14 pounds

FOR BRINE

Boiling water, 2 tablespoon

Red pepper flakes, 1 tablespoon, crushed

Kosher salt, ½ cup

Water, 18 cups

Thyme springs, 4

Granulated sugar, 1 tablespoon

Peppercorns, 2 tablespoons, crushed

Vegetable oil, ½ cup

FOR SEASONING:

Chili powder, 1 ½ tablespoons

Garlic salt, 3 tablespoons

Unsalted butter, 8 tablespoons, melted

Ground black pepper, 1 ½ tablespoons

Thyme, ½ bunch

Sage, ½ bunch

FOR DRESSING:

Extra virgin olive oil, ½ cup

Ground black pepper

Chives, 6 tablespoons, finely chopped

COOKING DIRECTIONS:

1. Add the pepper flakes and boiling water in a bowl. After 2 minutes, include this mixture in a large bowl along with all the brine ingredients. Slowly keep stirring until all the salt and sugar get dissolved. Leave it for 1 day, then, remove all the solids from the brine.

2. Carefully carve the bird with a boning knife. Make sure you don't damage the skin while doing this. However, it is also possible to smoke the turkey along with the bone and break afterwards.

3. Take a big sealable bag to pack the whole turkey and add all the brine in the bag along with it. After pouring the brine, carefully seal the bag and refrigerate for ½ or 1 whole day.

4. Get your Kamado ready for smoking at 275 degrees F.

5. Take the bag of the turkey out and pat dry it with the help of a clean towel. Then, carefully coat the whole turkey with vegetable oil.

6. Shift the turkey over the Kamado and smoke until the thickest internal temperature reaches 165 degrees F. If you have placed the thermometer in the breasts, then, it should indicate 155 degrees F. This will take about 3 to 4 hours. However, the big birds might take more than that.

7. While the turkey is getting smoked, you can work on the seasoning. Combine all the ingredients.

8. When the turkey gets ready, remove it from the Kamado and butter it on each side with the help of the herb. Then, use your hands for seasoning the skin on every side of the bird.

9. Cook it again for about 1 hour until the thigh temperature reaches 175 degrees F.

10. Prepare the cutting board by pouring a little amount of the olive oil, pepper, and chives. Then, shift the turkey from the Kamado to the cutting board and leave it there for 15 to 20 minutes.

11. After that, you can start slicing the meat. Serve the meat on a plate by using the pepper and other ingredients to garnish.

SMOKY CHICKEN IN SPANISH STYLE
INGREDIENTS TO PICK:

Chicken, 4 to 5 lb, whole

Lager beer, 1 can

Chorizo sausage, 4 oz

Lime, 1, cut into 8 pieces

Ancho chili, 1, dried

Sweet paprika, 1 teaspoon, smoked

Chili powder, ½ teaspoon

Cumin, ½ teaspoon

Granulated garlic, 1 ½ teaspoon

Cayenne pepper, 1 teaspoon

Sea salt, 2 tablespoons

Onion powder, 1 ½ teaspoons

Olive oil, 2 tablespoons

Ground black pepper, 1 tablespoon, fresh

COOKING DIRECTIONS:

1. Open the can of lager and mix small pieces of lime, dried ancho pepper, onion and black pepper. Then, shake it well to prepare.

2. Now, take the chicken and add the chorizo inside the skin carefully. Save a little amount of chorizo and put it inside the neck section.

3. Prepare the mixture of garlic, onion powder, cumin, cayenne pepper, salt and pepper, chili powder also. Rub this mixture all over the chicken, place the lager can inside the carcass of the chicken, and shift it on a foil pan. This will collect all the drippings from the chicken.

4. Now, shift the pan in the Kamado and smoke it for about 2 to 3 hours. Make sure that the temperature is about 310 to 325 degrees F.

5. Get rid of the can after cooking and leave the chicken for about 15 minutes. Then, make two equal pieces by cutting and serve it with salad and veggies.

MEXICAN ROASTED CORN
INGREDIENTS TO PICK:

Corn, 6, unhusked

Mayonnaise, 6 tablespoons, divided

Chili powder

Parmesan cheese, ½ cup, shredded

Lime, 1 wedge

COOKING DIRECTIONS:

1. Prepare the Kamado at the preheat temperature of 350 degrees F.

2. Start roasting the corns and keep on doing it for about 30 minutes.

3. Leave the roasted corns for about 5 to 6 minutes for cooling.

4. After cooling, pull out all the husks from the corns downwards. Let the base attached.

5. Rub the butter and mayonnaise over the mildly warm corn ears. And also sprinkle the cheese and chili powder. Finally, add lime juice and serve.

ROASTED LAMB CHOP WITH MINT SAUCE
INGREDIENTS TO PICK:

Lamb chops, 1 rack

Garlic clove, peeled and smashed

Grapeseed oil

FOR SAUCE:

Apple cider vinegar, 1 cup

Fresh mint leaves, 1 cup

Lemon juice, 1 teaspoon

Confectioner's sugar, 4 teaspoon

COOKING DIRECTIONS:

1. Prepare the Kamado for roasting at about 200 degrees F. Let it get ready for about 20 to 30 minutes, and then, increase the temperature to 350 degrees F for next 20 minutes of cooking. The final cooking temperature should be 450 degrees F for the 20 minutes. Hence, it will take about 60 minutes of preparation.

2. Pat dry the lamb and rub the chops with smashed garlic. Also, add the grapeseed oil with the help of a brush.

3. Now, cook the chops for about 5 to 6 minutes and then shift them back on the cutting boards.

4. Cover the chops with foil and leave it for about 10 minutes.

5. Mix all the sauce ingredients in a food processor. See when the mint gets chopped properly, then, include the lemon juice and keep it in the refrigerator. When you want to use the sauce, take it out and leave it at the room temperature for a while.

6. Pour the sauce over the lamb chops and serve.

ROASTED HALIBUT WITH TOMATO RELISH
INGREDIENTS TO PICK:

Halibut, 2 pounds, fresh fillets

Kosher salt, according to taste

Black pepper, according to taste

Red wine vinegar, 2 tablespoons

Canola oil, 2 tablespoons

Feta cheese, 3 ounces, dry

Kalamata, olives, 10 ounces, sliced

Red onion, 1, diced

Garlic cloves, 3, minced

Tomatoes, 14 ounces, diced

Extra virgin olive oil, ¼ cup

COOKING DIRECTIONS:

1. Mix all the ingredients except for the halibut. Refrigerate this prepared mixture for about 3 to 4 hours.

2. Prepare the Kamado for the roasting process at a temperature of about 400 degrees F.

3. Use salt and pepper for the seasoning of the fish fillets.

4. Roast the halibut in the Kamado for about 9 to 10 minutes. Use a fork to check when the fish starts flaking.

5. Fish is ready now. You can put a little amount of the tomato blend on it and let the fish get a little warm with the tomato relish.

6. Now, shift the fish to a serving plate, add more tomato relish and serve.

STEAMED TAI SNAPPER (WHOLE)
INGREDIENTS TO PICK:

Tai snapper fish, 1 lb, whole

Lemon, 1, thin slices

Wakame seaweed, 2/3 cup, cut into pieces

Mushrooms, 3 oz

Your favorite sauce

COOKING DIRECTIONS:

1. Start by seasoning the fish on every side. Leave it for about 20 to 30 minutes.

2. Use a paper towel to carefully pat dry the fish, then, put the slices of lemon inside the cavity.

3. Prepare the Kamado for steaming by using the manufacturer's steaming instructions.

4. Place the fish over the wakame seaweed and steam for about 8 to 9 minutes. Make sure you keep the dome closed during the steaming.

5. Now, take out the fish and shift it to a serving plate. Garnish with the lemon slices and mushrooms. Enjoy the steamed fish with your favorite sauce.

STEAMED PORK WITH GREEN VEGGIES
INGREDIENTS TO PICK:

Pork, 8 oz, sliced and cut

Cabbage, 5 oz, stripped

Bean sprouts, 5 oz

Mushrooms, 5 oz

Carrot, 2 oz

Salted water, 2 tablespoons

COOKING DIRECTIONS:

1. Use the salted water to mix the pork slices. You can use your hands to properly mix the pork slices. Then, leave the slices to refrigerate for about 30 minutes.

2. In the meantime, you can prepare your Kamado according to the steaming instructions given by the manufacturer.

3. Put a steaming grate over the Kamado and create a bed of cabbage for the pork slices. However, before adding the slices you need to place carrots, sprouts, mushrooms in layers. Then, you can place the pork slices at the top of the veggies.

4. Now, it is the time to cover it and let it get steamed for about 9 to 10 minutes. Make sure that the meat is cooked when you take it out.

5. Finally, carefully take it out on a serving plate and serve it with your favorite sauce.

STEAMED CHICKEN IN TEA FLAVOR
INGREDIENTS TO PICK:

Chicken, 16 oz, boneless

Tea leaves, 1 tablespoon

Salt, 1 tablespoon

Ginger, 1 knob, sliced into tiny pieces

Water

FOR SAUCE:

Soy sauce, 2 tablespoons

Black vinegar, 2 tablespoons

Garlic, 1, grated

Honey, 1 teaspoon

Ginger, 1 teaspoon, grated

Sesame oil, ½ tablespoon

White sesame seeds, 1 teaspoon

COOKING DIRECTIONS:

1. Take the chicken and use your hands to season it with salt. After complete seasoning in all sides, carefully place it in the refrigerator for about one night.

2. Boil the water and use it to soak the tea leaves. It will take about 5 to 6 minutes for complete soaking. Then, take out the leaves and slowly drain the water from it.

3. Mix the tea leaves with the ginger slices using your hands. '

4. Prepare the Kamado for the steaming according to the manufacturer's instructions.

5. Place a steaming grate over the Kamado and cover it with a parchment paper.

6. Over the paper, you need to spread about the half of the tea leaves. Then, place the chicken on the tea leaf and ginger mixture spread on the paper. Finally, pour the rest of the mixture carefully over the chicken.

7. Cover the dome and steam for about 12 to 13 minutes. Make sure you keep an eye on the chicken. Take it out when the chicken is completely cooked.

8. During the steaming, you can prepare your sauce. Combine all the sauce ingredients in a medium-sized bowl and mix them together.

9. When the chicken is ready, shift it back to a cutting board and start removing the tea leaves. Make sure you remove all the leaves. Now, use the cooking juice to pour over the chicken and pour the vinegar sauce. Ready to serve!

STEAMED CHICKEN DUMPLINGS
INGREDIENTS TO PICK:

Ground chicken, 14 oz

Potato starch, 1 tablespoon

Soy sauce, 1 teaspoon

Sesame oil, 1 teaspoon

Ginger, ½ tablespoon, grated

Dumpling wrappers, about 20 to 25 pieces

Black pepper, according to taste, freshly ground

Cabbage leaves, 4 to 5, wide pieces

COOKING DIRECTIONS:

1. First of all, you need to start by preparing the filling for the dumplings. For that, you can take a large bowl and include all the ingredients except the dumpling wrappers. Properly mix the ingredients together with your hands. Then, wrap with plastic and leave this mixture for about 30 to 45 minutes in the refrigerator.

2. Now, you can start working on the Kamado preparation for the steaming. Put the steaming grate over it and set according to the manufacturer's instruction.

3. Take out the mixture from the refrigerator, and start making the dumpling wraps. You need to fill the optimum amount of mixture only over the wrap. Make sure there is enough wrapping left to seal the mixture. Then, use water to carefully seal the wraps.

4. After preparing the dumpling wraps, you can shift them over the parchment covered plate. Also, cover the dumplings with a paper towel.

5. To prepare the steaming, you need to place the cabbage pieces over the steaming grate. Then, close the dome and let the cabbage pieces get a little softer.

6. Now, you can carefully arrange the dumplings over the cabbage pieces and close the dome to steam it for about 6 to 9 minutes. Check whether the chicken is cooked or not.

7. Take out the steamed dumplings and serve with your favorite sauce.

JAPANESE STEAMED CLAMS
INGREDIENTS TO PICK:

Clams, 16 to 18 oz, scrubbed

Garlic, 1 clove, thin slices

Olive oil, 1 tablespoon

Red chili pepper, 1, dry

Soy sauce and salt, 2 tablespoons, for seasoning

Salt, according to taste

Lemon, a few wedges

Rapini, 5 oz

COOKING DIRECTIONS:

1. Add the garlic pieces and chili pepper into a pan and cook for two minutes at a medium temperature. Make sure that the aroma of the spices start coming out, then, immediately stop cooking.

2. Now, take all the clams and cover the cooked spices with it. After that, cover the clams with the rapini leaves until it gets completely covered.

3. Finally, you can shift the pan over the Kamado for steaming. Cover the dome and let the clams get steamed for about 4 to 5 minutes.

4. After the steaming of 5 minutes, you can take out the clams and add a little extra salt according to your own taste. Carefully, mix the salt with the clams.

5. Finally, pour some lemon juice over the clams and serve immediately.

ABOUT THE AUTHOR

James Houck is a health and fitness enthusiast who loves teaching people about healthy ways to lose weight and live the best life they can.

Over the years, he has studied what works and what doesn't in health and fitness. He is passionate about helping others achieve great success in their diet and exercise endeavor through his books and seminars.

His biggest satisfaction is when he finds out that he was able to help someone attain the results they've been looking for. In his free time, he loves to spend time with his 2-year-old daughter.

CPSIA information can be obtained
at www.ICGtesting.com
Printed in the USA
LVOW09s1314291117
557947LV00047B/69/P